ze
therapy

zen
therapy
healing your life with zen

Robert Milton Anthony
with J. Digby Henry

ARCTURUS

Arcturus Publishing Limited
26/27 Bickels Yard
151–153 Bermondsey Street
London SE1 3HA

Published in association with
foulsham
W. Foulsham & Co. Ltd,
The Publishing House, Bennetts Close, Cippenham,
Slough, Berkshire SL1 5AP, England

ISBN-13: 978-0-572-03211-1
ISBN-10: 0-572-03211-0

This edition printed in 2006
Copyright © 2006 Arcturus Publishing Limited

British Library Cataloguing-in-Publication Data: a catalogue record for this
book is available from the British Library

Printed in China

Contents

Preface

Out of needs for beginnings,
we create gods.

With desires for immortality,
we enthrone them.
In avoidance of spontaneity,
we obey them.
In fear of risk,
we follow them.
From rejection of responsibility,
we worship them.

This pre-tension
protects us
from the tension and consequences
of our choices and actions.

We must learn
to enspirit our lives
and live out our inner deity.

Introduction

This book is not about any thing
or any one.

It is a creation and a reflection
of Zen Transactional Therapy,
offered in memory of no one,
dedicated to no one,
written for no one,
with a premise that whatever
you take seriously is your master,
and whatever you master
has no need of your seriousness.

We present this to you gently,
as a *koan* to be solved,
with a smile and plenty of laughter.

Robert Milton Anthony, Ph. D.
J. Digby Hunt, M.A.

The principles of Zen
Transactional Therapy (ZTT)

Zen (Z)

The active process
of a person's unification
with all-that-is,
where no thing
and no one
has more importance
than any thing
or anyone else.

Transactional (T)

The creative interplay
of the world
with the world,
wherein all are affected
by the play and its consequences.

Therapy (T)
The enrichment
of all persons and their lives through
humorous play,
creative game-playing,
tension exploration,
socio-inspection,
preferential relating,
wherein each person is a priority
over all else.

ZTT
A crucible of creative life.
Rather than living life and playing ZTT,
one plays life and lives ZTT.

Zen master

A living portrait
of all that fulfils your fear
of being spontaneous.
Beacon and signpost,
twinkling with laughter,
dancing in your path.
The master plays life to its fullest.

In words and actions, he invades
your victimhood
with an invitation to play beyond
the boundaries of your own drama.

The master seeks no followers
and does not dictate,
possessing no one and subjugating
no thing.
The master imposes neither himself
nor the therapy
upon anything or anyone.

Pilgrims

A pilgrim came to the master asking,
'How can I discover who I am?'

Eyes twinking and laughing,
the master replied,
'When you find the difference between
an apple, you will discover who you are.'

Another pilgrim came to the master
saying, 'I don't know what is wrong.
I am not myself today.'

'Then,' said the master, 'since you are
not you, to whom am I speaking?'

When the butterfly
rests in your hand,
do not close it.

The principle of infinite identity

A picture frame serves a two-fold
purpose: to include all that is in the
picture and exclude all else. The frame
you place around your life defines you
and excludes all the possibilies of who
you are and who you can be.

The reach of who you are
includes your unique self (core identity)
and all else around you (corporate
identity). Your allegiances are to the
universal and the cosmic.

The search for one's identity
is a quixotic fantasy.
One's identity already exists
and must be accepted
before it can be changed.

Conquering the enemy within

The narcissistic insular ego
(the serpent slithering into the self)
poisons its well.

You are who you are, cannot but be
who you are
unless you choose to change.

Physiologically,
biologically,
genetically,
historically,
socially,
you are unique.

Do not worry when you incorporate
the experiences of the other
into your own identity
You cannot lose what
you cannot give up.

Whatever you are doing,
become one with it.
Whoever you are with,
become one with them.

Who you are, who you are with
changes from moment
to moment.

Do not set in concrete
any impression of yourself
or of another
as the final representation
of who you or they are.

We are growing, moving, changing –
interpersonal acts
in the theatre of life.

Within and without

Your identity includes all that is –
within and without.
Everyone and everything is
an aspect of your identity.
It is all part of you.
To say 'this is not me' is
an illusion of words
supported by an insular identity.
When you isolate and insulate
your experience
(from all other experiences),
you countenance the maquerade
of loneliness.

Being one with others

The more you practise
the attitude of unity
with others,
the more you will sense
the experience of unity.

It does not require that
the other person
have the same vision as you.
When both experience unity
with each other, there is joy
and a sense of corporateness.

Open and extend
your family to include
all beings.

Pulling down the walls
of separation

Reflex and automatic responses
are walls between people.
Learn not to act out
every distressing feeling or emotion
stimulated by others.

When not supported in action,
these feelings or emotions disappear
in the flow of mutual interaction.

With each person you encounter,
you move towards intimacy of experience
but intimacy of action requires
mutual agreement.

Intimacy of experience is the product of mutuality.
Mutuality arises from the activity
of each person experiencing the other
in the present moment.

Looking into another

In complete mutuality
I look at you and see you
you look at me and see me

In pseudo-mutuality
I look at me and see me,
you look at you and see you.

In incomplete mutuality
we look at an issue or a cause
and create the illusion
of togetherness.

Intimacy of action
and the mutual agreement
to act on the basis of what both
see, feel and wish to do.
Mutuality requires
the commitment to challenge
one's own vulnerabilities.

Capturing the here-and-now

To bring yourself
and the person you are with
into the present moment,
focus your attention on the other,
be aware of what you both
sense, experience, wish to do.

Begin this process of socio-inspection with
your attention focused on the other and
complete these statements:

'I see you ...' *(Give an impression.)*

I see you ... and feel towards you ...'
*(Include those feelings which are based
on your impressions.)*

'I see you ... and feel towards you ... and I
would like ...' *(Give a statement of desires or
actions based on your impressions and feelings.)*

The mutability of
human impressions

As your impression of another
changes from moment to moment,
so what you feel and wish to do
also changes.

Socio-inspection is the activity
of treating oneself as background
and others as figures.

Become socio-inspective in
your relationships,
allowing others and their issues
to figure in the response
where you are the background.

Only in this manner
can you truly
be with one another.

Avoiding self-isolation

Do not set your experience in concrete.
Do not attack or defend impressions,
feelings or desired actions when with another.
Such behaviour isolates you and wards
off mutuality.

Through a child's eyes

They mirror who you are, what you are,
how you are, and what you avoid in the world.

Crafty living

You are a craftsman in the theatre of life,
learn to be an effective manipulator.
Treat yourself and others as moving sculptures
evolving into ever more complex forms.

Enhanced self-awareness

A process of checking in
on oneself, taking care
that oneself does not interfere
with one's blending with another.

Treading life's stage

To be fully who you are,
become the actor or the actress
and play out in total
the person you want to be
because action changes being.
Being and becoming
are one and the same.

Infinite identity

Cosmic scales

No person has more or less value
than any other person in the universe,
or any living entity in the universe,
or the universe itself.

Tipping the scales
of the cosmos

In a world
where all people and all things
are equally important,
people still have priority.

When they do not,
they are brutalized,
each becoming
some thing instead
of someone.

A fair trade-off

To act in preference and priority
does not require the devaluation
of that which is not preferred.

Life's prism

You and I are one facet
of all-that-is.
All others are too.
They are you, you are they.
I/you/they/we are all-that-is.

All-that-is
is all-that-is.
It is reflected everywhere,
in everyone
and everything.
It is, was and will be, always.

The principle of humorous play

'There is no joy in my life,' said the pilgrim. 'Show me how I may find happiness.' The master smiled, and laughed and laughed and laughed, and then he laughed some more.

Divine mirth

Everything is sacred
and there to be laughed at
with the irreverent humour
of one free from fear and constraint.

Laughter dissolves tunnel vision
and increases the options of choice.

Learn to laugh
in the face of seriousness.
Act humorously
where seriousness directs your course,
and seriousness will melt
into joyous experience.

Laughter remedy

To discover humour,
you need to act with humour,
even when you do not feel
humour inside.

Laughter is the transport
through the barriers
of emotional pain.

ZTT laughter is never used for derision
but for incorporation with all-that-is.

Confusing compulsion

Compulsive expressions of strong emotion
are often confused with spontaneity –
the light, humorous, caring result of
having learned to act independently of
negative and positive emotion.

Spontaneous humour

Spontaneity results
from self-discipline.

Discipline yourself
to play humorously
at home
in work
at play.

Everywhere
and everything
is a playground
for humour.

Discipline
without
joy
is fatal.

The influence of others

Beware the seriousness of others.
Contagious and addictive, it makes you
you lose concern for mutual enrichment
becoming entrenched
in an impoverished, insular identity.

Laugh whenever possible,
and play at being serious.

Rediscovering childhood

If you have forgotten the creative,
explorative, curious freedom
of childhood, play children's games.

Peek-a-boo is an incredible game
to play with adults,
especially when the other person
is drowning in seriousness.

The tragedy of being serious

Those who cannot choose
to play the fool are condemned
to live as caricatures.

Laughter's tale

The problem of laughter
is best resolved
by laughing
at the problem.

Your enemies are really
  your friends

Delight in those who make you angry.
They are your friends, those who point
to the vulnerabilities that continue
to make you a victim.

The search for happiness

Happiness is not to be sought.
It is a by-product
of humorously solving
human problems
and a consequence
of continuously
eroding the barriers
to experimental intimacy.

The principle of tension exploration

'I feel like a doormat,' announced another pilgrim on his arrival.

'Everyone treats me like a doormat! What should I do?'

'Practise being a doormat to the fullest, until you are the best doormat,' replied the master, 'then you may discover there is no question.'

Pain avoidance (1)

Those feelings defined
and understood
as negative
are always experienced
as painful.

Change the definition
and the pain softens.

It is often
manifestly easier
to remain secure
in anger and depression
than to risk
the threatening uncertainty
of change.

Pain avoidance (2)

Most people are tension-reductive
with themselves and with others.

In reducing the tensions of experience,
they avoid pain automatically,
often becoming quite angry
and destructive when pressed
into the experience of their agony.

Any experience or activity
which serves to avoid tension
becomes quite addictive.

Addiction and avoidance
become coercive directors
in living, working, playing,
thinking and fantasizing.

Beware of extremes

Addictive behaviour creates extremes:
emotional highs and lows.

These, too, are addictive.

Beware the emotional
shield of escapism

Fantasy can be a tool or a tomb.

The ultimate avoidance
is found in the
isolated security
of fantasy
and psychosis.

Face as much emotional pain as possible.
The more you face,
the less there is.

Feeling out of touch

When you are out of touch
with yourself,
your feelings and emotions
and ongoing sensory experiences,
seek out any therapy through which
you can achieve
a healthful self-awareness.

Otherwise, you will have
serious difficulty becoming
a warm, sensitive person
with yourself
and with others.

Automatic emotional responses

Guilt,
shame,
anxiety,
jealousy,
possessiveness
and embarrassment
are automatic emotional responses.

Do not act
on the basis
of these.

Experience them fully;
then act with choice
and preference.

Rebuilding your inner child

Through the travail of childhood
people too often lose
their responsive joy
and attentive enquiry
with the surrounding world.

To restore these as adults,
they must pro-act:
play out joy and attentiveness
in conscious choice and struggle.

Those unwilling to face
their own pain
will inevitably
inflict it on others.

Separating what's yours
from what's theirs

Let others be responsible
for their own behaviour,
not for your feelings or emotions.

Acknowledge your feelings
and emotions
as your own.

Beware those
who would protect you
from your own experiences.

The skill of the struggle is your inner
ability to choose to explore
the tension of your experiences.

What's in a lifestyle?

Most lifestyles, from normal to psychotic,
conventional to radical,
are cartoons and caricatures,
conducted automatically
without conscious choice.

First impressions

Your first impression of someone
will automatically tell you how
that person responds
to you and to others.

The initial contact is often
an automatic, promiscuous activity,
avoiding unfamiliar distress,
discomfort and emotional pain.

Outside your comfort zone

The direction to take in any relationship
is towards the behaviour, feelings, emotions
and topics which are most uncomfortable.

The benefit of
sharing weaknesses

Share your vulnerabilities with
other people as often as possible.

Consider those your friends
who for your sake
stimulate and caricature
your emotional hurts.

Act reverently towards them
they point to the restricting walls
of your life and invite you to move
beyond those walls.

Fellow travellers

Those you live with and are close to
are potentially your finest therapists.

They instantly know
your vulnerabilities
and are best able
to stimulate them.

Life should never be
a spectator sport

By avoiding their vulnerabilities,
most people make life a spectator sport.
Beware those who pride themselves
on being 'real' people.
They usually take themselves
and their words quite seriously,
becoming deadening when not taken
seriously by others.

Inner release

Consider yourself
a riverbed
over which
positive and negative
experiences flow.

Observe them
but do not enmesh
yourself in them.

They are the indicators
not the directors
of your life.

Do not cling
to negative feelings and experiences
in morbid introspection.
Let go your hold
on positive feelings and experiences.

When the butterfly
rests in your hand,
do not close it.

Does intensity make it real?

The intensity of your emotions
does not make a right.
The intensity of your actions
does not make a truth.

Changing direction

When changing who you are,
rely on your actions and your intellect,
not on your feelings and emotions –
they are too capricious.

Rising up from the ashes

Tension exploration
fires the 'phoenix effect',
a recreation of the self.

Self-analysis and observation

With your experiences
be an anthropologist

Observed, undisturbed,
they will go their own way.

Watched, untouched, they will pass on
in the flow of the now.

The pleasure of one's own company

Be with yourself like the potter
with wheel and hands
centred in the present moment,
forming the clay
of your own being
into thousands of complex designs.

Setting the wheels of change in motion

Each person
is an actor or actress
in need of self-change.

Self-change requires
the acts of 'as if'.

You may act 'as if' to expand
who you are or you may act
'as if' to prevent changing
who you are!

An attitude of self-change
or self-protection:
it's a constant choice.

To act 'as if'
is to choose
your behaviour.

The principle of transactional game-playing

The master came upon a man beating a child. 'To what end do you brutalize this child?' he enquired. 'My son here hit his smaller sister. He is a bully and I am punishing him!' came the angry reply.

'Oh!' said the master, 'I see ... you are showing him how to be a better and angrier bully.'

Self-definition

You are defined by
words,
actions,
feelings,
emotions,
fantasies,
images
and thoughts –
the tools
and aspects
of your being.

Left unattended,
they will
direct, manipulate and control
you.

Life's steward

In living, you are the steward of your
words, actions, feelings,
emotions, fantasies, images
and thoughts.

How you develop these
determines the course
of your relationship
with yourself and with others.

A passage framed
only in feelings, emotions and fantasies
creates a life
fraught with experiential pain
and cynicism.

A journey directed by choice and action
fulfils the self and creates joy.

Strengthening the self

In order for all feelings and emotions
to continue, they must be
strengthened by words,
actions,
fantasies,
images
and thoughts.

Speak, act, imagine and think
as the person
you want to become.

What you are becoming
is who you are.

Waffits

These are
words,
actions,
feelings,
emotions,
fantasies,
images and
thoughts.

Whether
they be
positive or negative
is determined
by you.

Spreading the word

You are responsible
for no one
and *to* everything.

It is our charge
to enlighten others
about their destructiveness,
sketching out their course,
modelling their possibilities.

Personal exchanges

In each transaction
with another
you create
a living art form
reflecting who you are.

Responsibility pledge

I am responsible to you
but not the master
of *your* behaviour,
emotions and feelings.

Do not allow me
to be the master
of your behaviour,
emotions and feelings.

I am the master
of *my* own behaviour
and emotions and feelings.

If we *both* are masters of our own
behaviour, emotions and feelings,
we have a good chance at
genuine mutuality and love.

Our responsibility towards others

By being 'responsible to others',
you encourage the creative,
experiential evolvement of their
independent being,
capable of empathic
and compassionate
caring for your self and others.

In being 'responsible for others',
you spawn their dependency,
narcissism, egocentrism
and callousness.

The 'responsibility to others' begins
with the birth of every child:
emotional and physical nurturing,
cleaning, clothing, housing,
protecting and fostering
spiritual evolvement.

If we as adults
are 'responsible for' rather
than 'responsible to' a child,
we are ensuring his or her
inability to create or experience
universal compassion and love.

The evolution of the spiritual
man or woman
begins with his or her taking responsibility
for his or her own being.

An invitation to yourself and to others

Be willing to experience
other people openly,
with no restrictions
on the experience.

If there are restrictions,
let them be theirs.

When you are with others,
let them be the focus
with you as the background.

Invite them to do likewise
and genuine mutuality will emerge.

You become what you do

In demeaning others, you become mean.
In brutalizing others, you become hateful.
In killing others, you become a killer.
In laughing, you become joyous.
In touching, you become close.
In loving, you become accepting.
In caring, you become compassionate.

Whatever you are is strengthened
by what you do, say, think, imagine
and fantasize about.
Even by default, you cannot escape
what you become.

Seeing through the haze

Like fools in a fog
people rely on feelings and emotions
for their life's direction,
believing the emotional haze
to be the limit
of themselves
and their world.

Ripples in the river of now

Choice directs action.
Behaviour begets feelings and emotions.
Look to your choices and actions
for the tools of change.

Your feelings and emotions
are only reflections and shadows
in the stream of your experiences.

The principle of preferential relatedness

Encountering a man striding
buoyantly down the street,
the master stopped him,
commenting on how awkward
he appeared.

The man's smile warped into
anger. 'What did you do that
for!' he cried. 'I was enjoying
myself until you came along.'

'It is a curious paradox,'
said the master gently,
'that to which you are
needfully attached is so
easily lost, and that which
you prefer is yours forever.'

Avoiding the pitfalls of attachment

When you are in need of others,
you become a victim to them
and to your needs.

That which you need controls you
becoming master and mistress
of your house.

Work to possess no one and no thing.
That which you possess directs you.

Seek to detach yourself
from all that attracts
and involves you.

That to which you are attached
controls you and it, not you,
determines the pathways of your life.

Caring for all living things

When you are with others by choice
you have no need
to control them
you are not in need
of any one thing
so are you truly free
to love and care
for yourself,
for all people,
for all living things
and for the universe.

Understanding non-attachment

Non-attachment
does not equal
non-commitment

One life

Each life is a drama
illustrating an array
of words, actions, feelings,
emotions, fantasies, images
and thoughts.

Let every kind of behaviour,
from conventional to psychotic,
traditional to radical,
whether yours or another's,
be an option in your repertoire
of possibilities.

Freedom is extant
in the potential
of all possibilities.

All around you are teachers

Each person
you encounter
is your teacher,
especially those people
you dislike or hate.
They, in particular,
present you with the opportunity
to free yourself
of your attachment
to hatred.

Let go of your anger
and irritation
towards others,
or you will walk
always in their shadow.

Reaching out to others

A most precious gift –
allowing others
to experience
your vulnerabilities
before reaching out
to touch their reality.

Cosmic relationships

Cosmic relationships
are not always possible.
Sometimes a cup of tea
together is all-that-is.

Recognizing when the gap is too wide

Because you and another
arrive at non-needfulness
in your relationship,
this is not an assurance
that your preferences will overlap.

Sometimes gears don't mesh.

At times, preferences and priorities
are different and they conflict.

Where the overlap of preferences
is not sufficient,
people cannot live together.

Creating relationships

There are these choices:
change it! *(first)*
live it! *(second)*
leave it! *(third)*

Relationships
are not found.
They are created.

The equal value of garbage and sunsets

Unless you grant equal importance
to garbage and sunsets,
you will be destructive
with those aspects of life
that you consider to be worthless.

Worlds away

That which you must avoid
and cannot be
(even in fantasy)
directs and controls you.

Practise imagining and creating fantasies
of the most awful and heinous acts
that could be done by you to yourself,
to others and to the world.

In the fantasy of these things
you can discover
the freedom not to do them
and escape the reflex act
of doing good.

Transcending limitations

The ability to lie
to stand free
from the imperative
automatic point of view,
is a first step in transcendence.

To step boldly beyond
the compassed cavern
of 'me' and 'mine',
into the unbounded
panorama of an absurd universe,
and there to create
all the facets of experience –
this is freedom laughing at the wind.

Time for oneself

At times, choose to be
away from others,
to experience yourself
alone in the non-person world.

Explore your loneliness whenever possible.
It is not a bottomless pit
but a bridge
to the experience of complete union
with the world.

Within aloneness rests the recognition
of one's singularity
integrated with all-that-is.

Sensuality and sexuality

Then came another pilgrim, blushing. He asked the master to speak of intimacy and sex. 'Ah,' said the master, nodding, 'you wish me to violate your preconceptions. That which must not be seen, cannot be looked at. That which must be kept silent, cannot be heard. That which must not be said, cannot be spoken of.'

Mutual consent

Sexual freedom
does not condone
sexual promiscuity.
It is directed towards experiencing
the uniqueness of the other
in an attitude
of common enhancement.

Closed relationships

Closed relationships
which forbid even
minimal emotional intimacy
with others around you
will become stagnant,
sequestered prisons
stifling all those involved.

Sowing the seeds of sexual preference

Once you have grown
through your sexual need
to develop and establish
your sexual preference,
you will discover
that there are many people
to share and enjoy this contact with.

Remember, the preferential heart
has many rooms!

A healthy sexuality
must be shared

Like any expression
of the human condition,
sexuality can be performed
in a context of caring and concern
for the other
or it can be isolated
and compartmentalized
within oneself alone.

When people become sexually aroused
they often become 'blind',
not seeing others
in all their assets and liabilities.

Sexual transference

Too often in sexual relationships,
people use each other
purely as objects
to satisfy desire.

Sexual relationships with people
of the same or opposite gender
have a real vitality
only when they are open
to the love,
sensuality
and sexuality
of others.

Open relationships

When experienced fully and released
an open relationship
must include
a willingness
to experience
and explore
the tensions of
stressful emotions
such as jealousy
and possessiveness.

When experienced fully
in the company of preferential actions,
these emotions give way to feelings
of mutual love and caring.

Sensuality vs sexuality

Preferential intimacy
brings to a relationship
the choice between
sensuality and sexuality.

Sensuality is interpersonal
and physical contact
without the necessity
of sexual activity.

It invites each person
into the intimate experience
of all feelings
between all people.

Publicizing the power of sexuality

Something
so powerful
and creative
as sexuality
should not
be hidden.

When love and sex
are openly explored,
people will
more actively
come to understand
what it means
to grow beyond
the purely physical boundaries
of their relationships.

The very private matter of sex

Most people
find it reflexively "natural" to
keep sex to themselves
or one other.

Needfully, they make it so,
defending their position
in anger and romance
with statements such as
'Sex is a personal matter' or
'The love between two people
cannot be shared with others.'

And the law?
Well, it mirrors the above.

Should we keep our sexual emotions and behaviour private?

Whether expressions of intimacy,
sensuality and sexuality
occur in the private or public domain,
and they should be for the people
involved to decide on as a matter of
convenience and preferential agreement.

As for the fear of adults
that children will be traumatized
by the physical expression of emotions
between two people in love –
When this love is the context of
    sexuality, what is the harm?

Tomorrow's world

In a socially evolved world
where people are
continually exploring
their own and others'
ways of being,
and are playfully
searching for
each other's vulnerabilities,
the sensitive depiction
of love and sex
would be a most
natural activity.

To close or not to close?

In an enlightened world,
the bedroom door
would ideally not be automatically
closed to children.

With children, what cannot be seen
and cannot be spoken about
is often relegated
to their fear-filled, magical fantasies.

Any human behaviour,
be it love, affection, hate, fear,
sex or death
which cannot be explored
in the healing light of day,
is remanded to the rituals
of ignorance, prejudice,
superstition and obsession.

In a sane world

In a sane and healthy society,
regular periods during work
would be dedicated to
expressing love, sex and affection.

In a mechanical world

In a push-button world
constructed from stress,
conflict and war,
the ongoing erosion
of human compassion
becomes the experience
of eternal disaster,
spawning depression, rage, revolution
and the reflexive rut
for the immediacy
of instant orgasm.

Death

Seeing a funeral, the master clapped
and cheered. 'Have you no compassion
for the dead?' one of the mourners
shouted angrily.

'The play is over,' mused the master.

Finding solace in the master

To the lost,
the master
is a beacon.

To the sorrowing,
the master
is a graceful
companion.

To the disconsolate,
the master
offers a gumdrop.

Life's a game

People often play their lives
automatically and seriously
without awareness.

They will employ
physical,
social,
political,
institutional
and legal powers
to win their games.

Serious automatic players
seldom play 'I win, you win' games.
Even less do they play
for the enjoyment of the relationship.

Beware of social conventions

Discover how seriously people
will perform their social conventions.
Respond to them
in a non-conventional manner
then beware!
They will blame you for 'hurting' them.
When you behave non-conventionally,
people will endeavour to stop you
with silence or disapproval,
blame and embarrassment,
coercion and threat,
demanding you stop playing games
become real and take them seriously.
This, too, is a game!

Yesterday, today and tomorrow

Use all of your experience
past, present and future
to facilitate
your involvement
with others.

However, do not allow
the ghosts and phantoms
of yesterday, today and tomorrow
to block the involvement.

Experience is a chain reaction

When you are with another,
no one exists except you
and the other.

Nevertheless, what you do
has experiential impact
for everyone, within and beyond
the immediate relationship.

As you and the other
affect each other,
so you stimulate the world.

Life lesson to the young

Teach your children not to kill.
That which is killed,
in the instant of death,
produces a killer,
and once dead,
can never reappear
for a living relationship.

The finger that pulls a trigger
is in all of us
and kills part of us
regardless of reason.

We are all interconnected

You are not independent
of what you do.
You are reflected in it
no matter what your
motive or method.

In bringing injury to another,
you bring injury to yourself.
You become what you do.

Should you ever kill another,
for whatever reason,
know that you have begun
the deadening of your own being.

Touching mortality

Death
is your constant
companion.

At any moment,
it may reach out
and touch
your mortality.

The enjoyment
of the world
is always
a shared experience.

The final passage

Death
is the common fate
of all living things.

None
may withhold
their passage.

The denial
of death
is the activity
of one approaching
winter with a match.

Recognizing emotional need

When disallowed, a need
is most clearly recognized
by its emotional accompaniment.
This orchestration of injury
will dissolve as the emotions are
experienced to their fullest in the
company of preferential behaviour.

Identifying a needy person

Conditioned emotional responses
are those feeling experiences
inevitably followed
or reduced by automatic
reflex behaviour.

These are the coercive characteristics
of the person in need:
obsessive, compulsive, reactive.

Awareness and self-change

Releasing the bondage
of negative feelings and emotions
is a most enlightening experience.

Know also that letting go,
even of physical pain,
releases the tears
and toxins of withdrawal.

A needful attachment
to one's strong feelings and emotions
erects permanent barriers to self-change.

Learn to experience each need
while acting in preference and choice.

When not acted upon,
need and its emotional cortège disappear.

Overcoming death

Gravity,
stiffness
and immobility
are all aspects
of the dead.

Laughter,
activity
and grace
are all manners
of the living.

Make humour, playfulness
and compassion
your companions in grief.

Days of open hand

Better an open hand
than a closed fist
in the face of death.

The task is one
of letting go
and reaching out
rather than
holding on
and fending off.

Understanding death

To equate death
only with loss
is to lose life
surely spring unfolds
only from the roots
of winter.

Birth and death
are the gates
to nature's garden.

Conquering worldly ties

Those who need to be
attached to the world
will always take life
and death personally.

ZTT game-playing

'I just want to be me!' announced the pilgrim emphatically. 'How can I be myself?' The master yawned and wrote the following prescription: 'Play at being you for one year. Play at not being you for the next year. If, at the end of these two years, you still have the question, play at being someone else since you obviously do not wish to be you.'

Playing ZTT (1)

Above all,
ZZT players school
in humour,
being able
to laugh equally
at themselves, ZTT
and the world.

ZTT players are socio-therapists:
active, humorous, preferential
players of life and living,
continually carrying out
a playful exploration
of their own and others' ways of being.

ZTT players (1)

In their adherence
to the principles,
ZTT players
actively hold
to the guidelines
of taking neither
themselves
nor ZTT

so seriously
as to be injurious,
so importantly
as to be coercive,
so righteously
as to be dogmatic,
or so concretely
as to be rigid
and unbending.

Playing ZTT (2)

ZTT is a meta-game.
It provides
a philosophical
and behavioural
framework
within which
all other games
are played.

That each of us
is game-playing
is not a new concept.

In ZTT, however,
the players
discipline themselves
to play kinetically,
manipulating without pause
to interrupt, disrupt

and change the course
of their own and others'
destructive game-playing.

ZTT players
are sensitive
to the levels
of reactive destructiveness
of others:
physically striking out,
instigating social, vocational
and legal retribution.
The degree of personal,
reactive destructiveness
is directly proportional
to the viciousness
of the retribution
all in the names of pride, honour,
social order, moral values
and sacredness.

ZTT players (3)

For a ZTT player
there are many ways
to interrupt
and play with
automatic, concrete
and reflex
ways of acting
and thinking.

For example,
explore and play humorously
with your own
and others' destructive
actions and speech
using the game tactics that follow.

Game tactics (1)

With compulsive talkers,
dismiss them with the statement that
what they are saying is unimportant.
If they begin to walk away,
tell them you have reconsidered
and ask them to return.
then dismiss them again.

With the constant complainer,
announce equal time
to voice your complaints.

With the chronically helpless,
announce that you are tired
of helping and that they must now
help you for a change.

Game tactics (2)

Exaggerate the other person's
gestures, tone of voice,
manner of speech or actions.

Create dissonance
in communications by
varying your verbal content,
eye contact, facial expression,
voice *(tone, volume, clarity and so on)*,
body posture, hand gestures
or physical distance.

Do these singly or in combination,
creating a humour-filled *koan*
for the other person(s) to solve.

Respond to the other with
definite pauses
or stuttering.

Turn your back to a person
who is communicating
destructively with you.

Abruptly excuse yourself
and walk away in the middle
of a conversation.

Game tactics (3)

In the face of seriousness,
laugh and continue laughing,
even if you don't feel like it.

Remember, humour
will follow laughter,
just as laughter
follows humour.

Mix in equal parts
serious and humorous responses
to any serious enquiry.

With the unending 'sad story' tellers,
begin an exaggerated sobbing,
and in tears tell them
that such a sad story
deserves all the pity in the world.

Game tactics (4)

Humorously describe
someone's reflex way
of relating
as 'psychopathology.'
Facetiously invite others
to practise this behaviour
so that they can learn how
not to do it.

With people who are always
having 'bad days',
ask them to give you
a detailed description
of how they create
such rotten days,
then invite them
to work harder
at creating
the best 'bad day.'

Game tactics (5)

With a group of people,
switch from person to person
in the middle of sentences,
changing the subject,
leaving each person with a
'hanging-in-the-air' *koan*.
Should anyone comment
on your rudeness, thank them
for the compliment.

To the complainer,
wonder aloud and mirthfully
as to why you must be subject
to such miserable conversations,
especially since you have evolved
to a higher plane of existence,
then ask why
this person is
punishing you
with his presence.

Games of disruption

Disruption games
are conducted
humorously,
with playful
and genuine concern
for the healthy
growth of all people.

The inability to play
humorously
can be attributed
to a defect
of the spinal column
known as
having a backbone.
Associated symptoms
are the stiff upper lip
and socks
that won't fall down.

Playing against 'contrariness'

It is equally important
to interrupt necessary attachments
to positive and good
feelings, behaviour
and experiences.

For example,
play seriously
at striving to create
a fun-filled, relaxing day.
Express dismay and sadness
that another feels so good.
Give them your condolences.

Play the role of 'contrary.'
Act contrary
to your positive feelings
for one day
then act contrary
to your negative feelings.

Play at being in a good mood.
laugh, smile and act happy,
regardless of how you feel.

Invite the ecstatic person
to do nothing until
the feelings of exuberance subside.

With the inevitable 'fun' person,
act bored.

Practise not needing

Remember, that which you need –
whether feelings, ideas, behaviour
or people – will inevitably control you.
Remember, you must expend energy
and concentration on satisfying
that need.

Compulsive
and needed
attachments
produce victims.

You become victim
of any behaviour,
thought or action
which must be compulsively
and automatically performed
to fulfil a need.

ZTT game-playing goals

A constant goal
in ZTT game-playing
is to create
the freedom to act
purposefully
from preference
rather than
from habit.

Because so much
of human contact
is conducted
automatically
with little thought
or feeling,
we are
too often
each other's habits.

To focus is to feel liberated

The experience
you compulsively
hold onto
imprisons you
in the fantasy
of what was,
and what might
have been.

Reflex and automatic behaviour
confine the flow of experience.

To remain unshackled
in the immediacy
of the present experience,
practise switching your focus.

Allow your attention
to scan the field
of experience
among and between
people,
situations,
events,
things,
thoughts,
feelings,
emotions,
fantasies
and memories.

That which
holds your attention
controls your attention!

Disrupting automatic fixations

To assist yourself and others,
disrupt any automatic fixations
that you may have,
switch the focus and fact
of your attention
in response to them
and the situation.

When next you are
in conflict with another,
switch the focus from your anger
to your appreciation
of the other person,
and share that with them.

People will often fix their attention
in the proper procedure
of a social convention
to avoid social tension.

The seriousness and rigidity
of avoiding tension can be interrupted
by taking the convention
and ritual literally
and humorously.

Playing with convention

Become playful
with convention,
for example,
before responding,
be as the child
who takes a long
and quiet,
unemotional look
at the other person.

Or accept the option to refuse
when a request is delivered
as a social question.

Perhaps shake hands
with the opposite hand
or not at all.

When asked, 'How are you?',
take hold of the other person,
thank them profusely for their enquiry,
and tell them how you are in detail!

This does not mean
every social convention,
rite and ritual
is tension-reducing
or is to be disrupted.

Beware those who take a guideline
and make of it an imperative rule.

The value of ten thousand words
is no more or no less than the actions
of their author or of their adherents.

Afterword

With each step
is the risk of falling.
In falling
is the possibility of loss.
In loss
is the discovery of awareness.
In awareness
is self-knowledge.
In self-knowledge
is the potential of being.
In being
is becoming.
In becoming
is movement.
In movement
is the risk of falling.
With each step,
a life unfolds
and returns.